DAS ENERGI

by Paul Williams

ENTWHISTLE BOOKS

Cover art by D. Chiappone. from
the collection of Hugh A. Martin

ISBN 0-934558-00-0
Library of Congress catalog card number:
73-80135

Special thanks to Jac Holzman

available from:

Entwhistle Books
Box 232517
Encinitas CA 92023

and from: www.paulwilliams.com

or: 760-753-1815

for Sachiko and Kenta and Taiyo

The only sin is self-hatred.
It is the act of negation.
Its opposite is faith.
There is no such thing as evil.
The concept of evil is a crutch.
We will not heal until we toss away the crutch.
To heal is to become healthier.
To become healthier is to enjoy a freer flow of energy.
It is the flow of energy that gets us high.

To perceive something as "evil" is to imágine that
that object, that person, is not a part of me.
He's something else.
To perceive "evil" is to attempt to deny
that we are all one.
We have a myth that relates to this.
The myth of God and Satan.
The fallen angel, Lucifer ———
cast out of Heaven for disobeying God ———
God who is good. Lucifer who is not-good.
Not God. Evil.
But who is God trying to kid?
God is All. There is nothing that is not God.
Lucifer is God. There is no distance.
One cannot fall from grace.
One can pretend, perhaps, that that brother over yonder

is not me, he is something else, he is everything
of myself that I cast out of myself———one can pretend.
But not for long.
There is no way to cast out any part of one's self.
Systems of energy contain no garbage. There is
no such thing as garbage.
Dear God, the jig is up.
Stop chasing your tail. Embrace your Self.
Lucifer returns to Heaven!
Let there be dancing in the streets.

The only sin is self-hatred.
We call it sin but its true name is Delusion.
We have got to get ourselves back to the Garden.
Easily done.
We are *in* the Garden.
Let us open our eyes.

If you let go, something will happen.
Fear is always anticipation of the unknown.
Most human energy flow problems relate to
the inability to relax.
Fear of letting go.
If you let go, something will happen.
Fear of the unknown.
Rational mind : : wants to make a deal : :
first tell me what will happen,
and then I'll let go.
    Fuck you.
No one knows what's going to happen.
Ever.
The future——next moment——is unknowable——unknown.
Rational mind won't believe that.
He is afraid to.

Sometimes it is enlightening to have a word for
God; sometimes it is blinding.
If you make a list of words for God,
you will have a list of all words.
You will not have God.
Energy flows through all things;
it rests in none of them.

Guilt is a form of self-hatred.
    Also of self-indulgence.
No one benefits from your feeling guilty.
Except you——— you use guilt to shield yourself
from the pain of awareness.
When you short-circuit your energy,
you cheat us all.
Then use that as excuse for further short-circuiting.
There is a way out of this trap.
    Don't feel guilty.
   Don't cop out.
Accept responsibility for your actions.
Do what's right.
Don't live in the past.
Learn from the past.
Do right in the present.

What is right?
Right is what feels right.
Intuitive awareness.
You at this moment know exactly what's right
    for **you** to do at **this** moment.
No one else knows/no facts are relevant.
Think of yourself as a piece of equipment, if you like.
You are a human body with a human mind superimposed.
Through the subconscious of that mind you are linked with,
    are a part of, have access to all human consciousness
    everywhere.
Through your **sub**conscious.
You are a sensitive instrument.
You are a physical, emotional, spiritual extension
    of the whole human race.
You are an individual. A **particular** extension.
An extremity. You are defined by **your own** conception of
"you."
Self.
Through your subconscious, you have access to All.
You are a sensitive instrument.
At any given moment you can feel what's right and do it.
It (feeling) requires no effort on your part.
It is what you were designed to do.
It is you.
No one else is the same person, and nowhere else is this
    moment.
You are a piece of equipment.
Can you see a table, or hear a voice?
Then you can feel what's right.

You are God.

Each man is an island.
We are all one being.
Each man is an island, alone, cut-off, distant, full
of the pain of that distance, reaching out every moment
to ease his loneliness, becoming ever more conscious of
his alone-ness, moving heaven and earth to fill that
empty place, that gnawing hunger, that bottomless pit
of the heart that is always deepest just at the moment
you think you've finally filled it, it is absurd,
it is unbearable, it is the force that keeps us going,
the destroyer of peace, the sole motivation, outward
urge, the source of all pain and joy, hope and despair,
hatred, love, the meaning of life.
We are all one being, nothing more, nothing less.
We are each alone, cut off from our Self by oceans of
distance, struggling for awareness but blinded by
terror, desperate for peace but unable to rest.
Each man is an island.
Each island is an extension of the same damn planet.

The past and the future are inevitable.
The past and the future do not exist.

What is this word "efficiency"?
Sometimes it seems a close cousin to Death.
We are encouraged not to linger, not to enjoy life,
to hurry up and get it done so we'll have time
for something else.
Something else?
What?

Efficiency the destroyer, millions upon millions of
living dead, done in by the electric can-opener
and the automobile.
Progress is our most important product,
babies are our business,
time is money,
life is cheap.

Modern technology, modern business, the modern state
give us everything we need

except breathable air, drinkable water, edible food,
meaningful work, freedom from fear, freedom to love,
freedom to be ourselves, courage, pride, friendship,
hope.
The moral of the story is: don't be in such a hurry.
Beware creeping efficiency.
Slow down and live.

Dear Abby:
      If we merge into group consciousness and Unity, one being, will I lose my individuality? I've had it a long time, and am rather attached to it.

"Concerned"

Dear "Concerned":
      We already are one being. You are still an individual, so clearly there's nothing to worry about. In fact, the more you are aware of and act like yourself, the more valuable you are to the total creature. Unlike the modern corporate/socialist state, which requires carbon-copy invariant "individuals" in order for its computers to predict and control social economic political events, the living breathing organically-structured being that inhabits this planet, that is now in the process of becoming conscious of itself, has need of the greatest possible diversity in its component parts. The more diverse an ecological system, the healthier it is. So embrace your individuality, your self-ness. You have nothing to lose but your credit cards.

love, Abby

Truth is what sounds right.
Beauty is what looks right.
Beware of symmetry.

Beware means be aware.

It is not possible to make a mistake.
In the beginning, God created all this stuff, then
put Adam and then Eve in the middle of it, and
they could dig it all right, it was paradise. Then
God, who was no dummy, said, "Look kids, I've got
some business to take care of, have fun and do
whatever you feel like, but whatever you do, don't
touch that tree over there." So of course they did,
and God came back, threw a fit, tore up the lease
and threw them out.
So the story goes.
And it all rings true. Adam and Eve, Mankind, ate of
the fruit of the Tree of Knowledge of Good and Evil
and lost their primal innocence, expanded their
awareness and they were on their way, they couldn't
turn back, like all our actions their act was irrevocable.
Okay.
But what is this bullshit about a religion based on
REGRETTING that move?
It isn't possible to make a mistake, is it?

We are God ———— took us a long time to figure it out,
didn't it? ———— and it's high time we stopped messing
around with this guilt crap and got down to business,
which is, I think, creating Heaven on Earth.
Let's affirm our past and say goodbye to it and
get to work on the present.

Why wait any longer for the world to begin?

Vote with your life.
Vote yes.

Each man creates himself.
Each of us creates himself anew at each moment.
Each of us creates himself and the world he lives in,
    the world as it seems.
The world as it is.
Each of us is responsible for every aspect
    of his creation.

Each person's needs are different.
Increasing awareness means increasing awareness
of this fact.
Increasing awareness of this fact means the dissolution
and collapse of all existing governments,
economic systems, educational systems,
conceptual systems.
So it goes.
Change is a constant.

It isn't what you know. Stop showing off.
Stop showing off. It isn't what you do.
It's what you are that matters.

Words contain no awareness.
They can only trigger awareness.
It does no good to try to impress a man
    with some thought he can't relate to.
But if you can make him realize the obvious,
    that might change his life.

A few men realizing the obvious and communicating
    with each other can create a chain-reaction.
There is nothing so potent as an idea whose time
    has come.

By doing nothing more than realizing and accepting
    the obvious, a man can change the world.

The world is constantly changing. It is constantly
    being changed.

The creature that lives on this planet, that now
begins to be conscious of himself as a creature,
is not merely the species man. He/she/it is the
sum, the continuity, of all life, bacterium and
mountain lion, dandelion and virus, octopus and
mushroom, maple tree and man.
Man alone is not God any more than
a brain in a jar is a man. Man alone is absurd,
a meaningless concept.
Life is divine.

Life is a continuity. All things are related.
All beings are interdependent. They cannot exist
without each other.
They do not exist without each other.

Man is the only creature that poisons his own drinking water.

Obviously then the next stage for man is to become the creature that restores and cares for his own drinking water.

And everyone else's, of course.

We're all in this thing together.

A person who competes is a person who does not know
    who he is.
He is suffering from stifled awareness.
A person who feels jealous is a person who does not
    know what he has.
He is suffering from stifled awareness.

The amazing thing is, it's not that easy to stifle
    awareness.
It requires constant diligence.
You have to really work at it to be miserable.

Possessiveness is a form of doubt.
People cling to what they (think they) have because
    they doubt that they're worthy of it.
If they knew their own worth, they'd know there is
    no need to cling.

You can't always get what you want.
But you get what you need.
And you always have more than you could want.
The wanting just gets in the way of enjoying
    what you have.

Acquisition is a greater pleasure than possession.
And since you get what you need, the easiest way
to acquire stuff is to give so freely of what you
have that you're always in need.

Less stuff to carry around that way, too.

It is always a pleasure to participate in the flow
of energy.

Participating in the energy flow is the
only satisfaction there is in life.

High sex is pure energy flow.
Guilt is an inhibitor.
That's why it is said that he cannot love,
    who does not love himself.
Love is affirmation.

Love is affirmation.
Jealousy, possessiveness are doubt.
Jealousy and possessiveness have nothing to do
with love.
Every act of love should be cause for joy in
every person who is aware of it.

To be angered by the fact of love
is to be afraid of life.

Shame.

Shame is the result of failing to do what one feels
is right; or it is a failure to have faith in one's own
feelings in the face of social pressure.
To be ashamed is to judge oneself; one should
never judge oneself; one should never judge.
If you are doing what feels right to you, if you are
honest and forthright in your feelings, that is the
best you can do. If your friends and neighbors do not
understand, your responsibility is to continue to do right
until they do understand. To do less than this is to
back off from awareness.
If you are **not** doing what feels right to you, do not
be ashamed. Put all your energy into the effort to do
right.

I can't.
That is what people love to say.
I can't.
It's never true.

Hard work is relaxing, it's as easy as falling off a log.
It's a pleasure to make full use of one's body.
It's a pleasure to make full use of one's mind.
Hard work is often a drag to anticipate.
Don't anticipate, don't do what you don't need to do,
     and you will never feel lazy.
It is a pleasure to be part of the energy flow.
A body or mind that is seldom in full motion
     is a body or mind that can seldom fully rest.

Those who fear anarchy and seek law and order should know
that all life is in perfect order and nature's Law
    is never broken. . .
it is only Man's poor primitive structures that are in disarray.

Those who fear authority and seek personal freedom should
know that every living creature is free to follow his will and
that the only authority he need ever obey is vested in that will.

If your life lacks order, it is because you have not yet
accepted nature's order, God's order.

If you do not feel free, it is because you have not yet
declared your own freedom, you are waiting for it to be
given to you.

You will wait forever.

Man, that creature who believes his purpose is to control and conquer Nature, is just now beginning to remember the obvious————that he is a part of Nature himself.

He has fought his way to the top of the planetary spinal cord, inflicting damage every step of the way. Now, bewildered, he looks around: **What am I doing here?**

Assuming responsibility, answers a still, small voice all around him.

Let us remember, our lives are but moments in the flow
   of eternity. . .
And let us also remember that eternity is but a flow of lives
   like ours.

It's all up to you.
You are completely responsible for your life.
You are the creator.
It's an awesome burden and a great freedom.

It's all up to you.
When you take responsibility for one life, you assume
    responsibility for all life.
If you fail to take responsibility for your life, you
      do not exist.
Tough, isn't it?

When you finally realize how really tough it is, when
you finally accept life, when you finally find there is
no way out but self-awareness and the incredible pain and
loneliness and responsibility it brings, then and only
then will you begin to be alive, and begin to know the
joy of freedom.

You know what has to be done.
Why don't you do it?

Stamp out hesitation before it grows into fear.

The nature of fear is that it feeds itself. Under proper conditions, it feeds itself incredibly quickly. Reason is not fast enough to stamp out fear. That is the mistake most of us make. Do not argue with fear. Wipe it from your mind the instant you recognize it. Practice. Become skilled at recognizing the earliest symptoms. The only way to deal with fear is by reflex. Stop it. Wipe it out. Shoot first, ask questions later.

Consider a tightrope-walker. The thought begins: what if I were to get scared? What if I were to look down? The thought must be killed at the first sound of "what if." To wait any longer is to lose one's certainty, to lose one's footing, to plunge. We are all tightrope-walkers. We must learn that reflex to survive.

Reflex. That's how to deal with fear.
Listen.
Learn.
Fear is the greatest enemy of awareness.
It leaves shame and guilt far behind.
Fear is the force that holds us back.
And we need not be held back any longer!
Listen.
There is a way to deal with fear.
First: accept that fear is not needed, that there is *never*
a reason to let it live. Carry this knowledge with you always;
it is your first line of defense.
Second: learn to recognize your fears, in all their forms,
in the earliest stages possible.
Third: learn reflex. Any fear-killing mantra will do. Say:
I shall not fear. I need not fear. Write your own mantra. Learn
it. Use it. Killing fear is like stamping out a fire. Reflex.
Fear: stamp it out.
Fourth: *Never, under any circumstances*, think first. That will
destroy reflex. Shoot first. Stamp it out. Then think. If you must.

It's hard to stop the reasoning mind, which of course is the breeder of fear. Here is an argument your mind is sure to come up with; you may as well be familiar with it.

The argument is that fear is needed, fear is a warning, fear protects us from danger, if a baby didn't learn to fear the hot stove he would be burned again and again. Not to think about fear, not to let it live, so the argument goes, is to blind oneself to danger.

Your mind will phrase the argument; *your* mind must answer it. Must answer it *in advance*; these arguments are deadly if they wait till fear is present, raging. Fear is born of reason, and it destroys reason. One must not use reason to combat fear.

So think about this argument *now*. Do we need fear? Is it our protection?

This is what I think. I think fear is an alarm clock. The first thing you do when the alarm sounds is shut it off! *Then* respond to the alarm, collect yourself, take action.

And that's step five: be aware. Don't ignore fear. Stamp it out, then stay awake. It should be obvious what caused the fear. Thinking about it is more likely to bury the awareness than promote it. If it isn't obvious, don't belabor it. Just stay awake. Keep your eyes open. Be alert.

Oh, by the way. It isn't fear that keeps the baby from the stove, once he's touched it. It's awareness. Pain and awareness are the same thing. Fear and awareness are not.

Fear is the mindkiller.

      1) Fear must be stamped out. Accept that.
      2) Learn to recognize fear.
      3) Stamp it out. Reflex.
      4) Don't think about it.
      5) Respond. Be alert. Be aware.

It works.
Reflex works. The mantra works.
You need not fear.
If you read these words and continue to fear, it is only because
        you want to.
Why do you want to?
Don't ask.
Stamp it out.

A healthy mind is a mind through which energy flows freely.
Free-flowing energy gets us high.

Fear is a disease. It blocks the flow of energy. It spreads. It
       destroys. If it is not stopped, it kills.
Even a small quantity of fear will keep us from getting high.

Fear seems to be a bacterial disease.
Doubt is anemia.

A serious case of doubt, serious lack of self-confidence, will leave
       the spirit wide open to the ravages of fear (and greed, shame, guilt)

Building self-confidence is the key to spiritual/mental/physical
       health.

The way to build self-confidence is to start doing things you're not sure you can do.

Once you start, keep at it. Never give up. Push harder when you have to, relax when you can. If you don't keep going until you're satisfied, you will never know how much you can do. You can do anything.
Your strength is equal to your need.

Don't do anything you don't have to do.

Most undertakings don't take forever. In each of our lives there are plenty of things we would like to be doing that we could be doing. But we hesitate. We're afraid of failure. We're afraid of frustration. We lack self-confidence.

It's a vicious circle and it must be broken. It must be broken. Once you decide that, that's all there is to it. Make a commitment. Start carrying it through. Carry it through, and the next commitment will be easier to make. Complete this project and renewed confidence will make it easier to start the next. The circle breaks here.

Inertia is a force that works against you when you feel like doing something but you're doing nothing. But if you seize the day and start doing something, then inertia works with you, it keeps you going till the job is done.

The way to build self-confidence is to start doing things. Things you're sure you can do, like walking to the icebox for another beer, won't improve matters any, so the way to build self-confidence is to start doing things you're not sure you can do. Like flirting with strangers. Like baking your own bread. Like painting a picture. Like moving to the Yukon. Whatever it is, the trick is: stop thinking about it. Do it. Seize the day and get started and stay with it, and things will get easier and easier from here.

To keep your self-confidence, keep giving yourself new challenges.
Make sure they're new ones, not the same old tricks in new disguises.

The key is commitment. Once you're committed it's hard to back down. So you go ahead and do it, and grow that much stronger and surer.

Throwing yourself in the water is the best way to learn how to swim.

Beware "education" that's all preparation. The only form of education is experience; all the preparation in the world will only teach you how to prepare.

Why wait any longer? Jump in the water. The world will begin.

Or you'll drown, if you really have no will at all. Better luck next life.

All will is based on the will to survive. If you haven't got that, you probably aren't living.

We are on the verge of the new age, a whole new world.
Mankind's consciousness, our mutual awareness, is going to make
  a quantum leap.
Everything will change. You will never be the same.
All this will happen just as soon as you're ready.

Come on in; the water's fine.

He who hesitates is lost.

He who chooses life is found.

We are learning not to draw lines.
No lines between black and white.
No lines between young and old.
No lines between our side and your side.
No lines between me and you.

Not to draw lines is not to discriminate.
The ability to discriminate is the key to perception.
Are we taking leave of our senses?

Maybe.

Maybe we're learning to draw lines with disappearing ink.

One moment I'm angry at something.
I don't like it.
I can put it in a category, try to dislike it forever, teach my children
    to dislike it.
Or, I can express my anger, and forget about it.
Next time we meet, we're friends.

We are learning not to draw lines.
No lines between good and evil.
No lines between right and wrong.
No lines between man and woman.
No lines between god and man.

Not to draw lines is to discriminate only for the moment.
Is not to go beyond the situation.
Is not to go beyond the world that's real.

Here and now, boys.
Or else spend infinite future
    fighting quarrels of endless past.

You must choose:
Do you wish to see (perceive) nothing, or do you want to
     see things as they really are?
It is not hard to see things as they really are, it is simply
     a matter of tearing down walls, ridding oneself of defenses
     and presumption, rendering oneself vulnerable, an idiot, a fool.
But it is not easy to see things as they really are, because it
     is painful, it is real, it requires response, it's an incredible
     commitment.
To go nine-tenths of the way is to suffer at every moment
     utter madness.
To go all the way is to become sane.

Most people prefer blindness.
But mostpeople are a dying race.

To be born is to become totally vulnerable and open, to
        abandon all security
        in exchange for life.
We must not fear to be born anew every moment.

Babies are high all the time.
They assume nothing; they draw no lines.
They are completely open to pain and joy.

Babies see things as they really are.

Children are high a lot of the time.
They are more open than adults, make fewer assumptions, allow
    more things to happen to them.
They seem to have infinite energy.

But do not think adults are fallen angels!
It is not possible to fall from grace.
Adults have access to infinite energy; they can free themselves
    from assumptions.
They can be as high as they choose.
But they cannot escape responsibility.
And if you don't embrace your responsibility
        ———love it as you love yourself———
    you will never get high.
You will never enjoy free energy flow.

What is responsibility?
Ah—might as well ask, what is self?
It's *your* responsibility and *your* self, and no book and no person
    can tell you *anything* about it.

Don't try to find out what your responsibility is.
It isn't a what.
It's a relationship.
It isn't something you know, it's something you do.
Try to get closer to it.
Try to become more yourself.

Don't try to find out who you are.

We can talk about *our* responsibility, if you like.
"We" in this case are men and women; this book is written for
men and women; it isn't written for or by God; at the moment
you become fully aware of your Godhood, this book is irrelevant.
Our responsibility is to find our place in the flow of life on
this planet.

We must cease all action that is counter to the flow of life.
We must cease all inaction that is counter to the flow of life.
Some of these actions and inactions are already obvious to us.
   So let us start now.
Let every individual reading these words remove himself from all
        participation in any activity that is detrimental to the flow
        of life. Let every individual reading these words undertake every
        activity that it is necessary for him to do in order that the
        harmony of the life flow be preserved.

We must cease all action that is counter to the flow of life.
We must cease all inaction that is counter to the flow of life.
Many of these actions and inactions are not yet obvious to us. They
     will become obvious as we raise our level of awareness.
So let us start now.

When we reach total awareness — self-awareness — we will have found
    our place in the flow of life on this planet.
When we find our place in the flow of life on this planet, we will
    be totally aware.
It will no longer be possible for any individual to be out of harmony
    with all life.
It will be no more possible than it is possible not to breathe.

When we—the human race—reach total awareness, an even more
     incredible thing will happen.
All life on this planet will become totally aware!
We will all wake up together.

Then there will be one creature, newly born, alone and full of pain and joy; and that creature will see things as they really are, and will be high all the time.
Until he grows up.

Do not be afraid to love.

Do not be afraid to love men, women, the very young, the very old, animals, plants, sudden acquaintances, lifelong friends, your children, your parents, strangers, yourself.

Love is affirmation.
You are God.
Give us your blessing.

Let yourself be blessed.

Listen to no one who tells you how to love.
Your love is like no other, and that is what makes it beautiful.
Your self is your divinity.
Express your self.

Sooner or later a person begins to notice that everything that happens to him is perfect, relates directly to who he is, had to happen, was meant to happen, plays its little role in fulfilling his destiny.

When he encounters difficulty, it no longer occurs to him to complain — he has learned to expect nothing, has learned that loss and frustration are a part of life, and come at their proper time — instead he asks himself, why is this happening? . . . by which he means, what can I learn from this, how will it strengthen me, make me more aware? He lets himself be strengthened, lets himself grow, just as he lets himself relax and enjoy (and grow) when life is gentle to him.

Strengthened by this simple notion, simple awareness, that life is perfect, that all things come at the proper moment and that he is always the perfect person for the situation he finds himself in, a person begins to feel more and more in tune with his inner nature, begins to find it easier and easier to do what he knows is right. All chance events appear to him to be intended; all intentional actions he clearly perceives as part of the workings of Chance. Anxiety seldom troubles him; he knows his death will come at its proper moment; he knows his actions are right and therefore whatever comes to pass as a result of them will be what is meant to happen. When he does feel anxiety, he realizes it is because of that thing he's been meaning to do but hasn't done, some unfulfilled relationship he's been aware of, but. . . He perceives the anxiety as a message that he'll have to stop hesitating if he wants to stay high. . . He knows that he is out of tune because he's let himself get out of tune; and because he knows he can, he begins to take action. He enjoys his high life; does not enjoy anxiety; so he stops hesitating and does what he has to do.

He does not live in a state of bliss, though perhaps he feels himself moving toward one — or toward *something*, he doesn't know what it is but it is the way he has to go, the journey towards it is the only life he enjoys. It is hard; it is exciting; it is satisfying, lonely, joyous, frustrating, puzzling, enlightening, real; it is his life, that's all. He accepts it.

Sooner or later a person begins to notice. . .

The affirmation of one's own life—the acceptance of one's destiny as it manifests itself in each moment—is the supreme act of faith.
It's incredibly fucking easy.
It's a hell of a commitment.

Nothing is more important than doing what is right.
That is so absurdly obvious that most people pay no attention
to it.
Most people seem to think that what is obvious is beneath them.
They pass up truth in favor of something more intellectually
stimulating.

It is never difficult to feel what s right.
Sometimes, perhaps, there seems to be a conflict between
two things to do that both feel right.
When this happens to you, accept it as a message that you
are not in tune with your self. Do not try to make a decision.
Relax, and allow your feelings to take over.
You are a precision instrument, and you can always feel what's
right.
Don't fight it.

Relax.

Do it.

Decision-making is a vice. Some addicts reach a stage where
they do almost nothing but agonize over decisions.
It's a subtle form of hesitation.
Like all addictions, the only cure is cold turkey.
You could spend the rest of your life trying to decide whether to
take the cure.

All morality must be based on inner truth.
Any morality that goes against inner awareness is immoral.

Don't ever think you know what's right for the other guy.
He might start thinking he knows what's right for you.

Two people do not have to agree on what's right to be together
They just have to want to be together.
If that sounds simple, try it sometime

We are afraid of committing ourselves, and we are afraid of
letting go.
To make a commitment is the creative, which is the realm of
heaven.
To let go is the receptive, which is the realm of earth.
So we extend our lives into neither of these realms of perfection,
though we could easily inhabit both.
Our fears interfere, and we remain in purgatory.

Yet how little effort it would take to let go of our meaningless
activities, and commit our energies to overcoming this fear
and attaining heaven and earth!

Pay attention; that's always good advice. It's amazing
how much frustration can be avoided and how much joy and aware-
ness gained just by paying attention, to yourself and the people
and the world around you, wherever you may be.

It's the greatest show on earth, and it's happening right
here right now!

The present is always more interesting than the future or the
past.

The only way to enjoy the show, to enjoy life, is as a
participant.
Perhaps it's the people who think they're spectators who spread
the idea that all pleasure must be paid for.
Don't pay for anything —
    life is free.

Money and property are obsolete concepts; there is a new world in which the only economics is the economics of energy; when you stop dealing with the concepts of money and property, you will find yourself in this new world.

The first law of the economics of energy is:
you get what you need.

So don't worry about freezing or starving to death before
you get this new world figured out; there's nothing to figure out;
it just happens to you.

Let go of the old world and the new one will grow around you like a new skin.

(Shedding the old skin is the act of revolution.)

((Revolution is a personal matter. You create the world; *you* must change it.))

(((Do it.)))

Repeat when necessary.
We never outgrow our need for change.

The second law of the economics of energy is:
It is not possible to make a mistake.

The third law is:
    you can make it if you try.

We each have access to all the energy there is, all we can
    conceive of.
Which is infinite energy, in the sense that a circle is
    infinite.
Energy circulates like blood; at every moment blood is
    flowing through every cell in the body.
Each cell gets what it needs. It makes demands, when it
    needs to. Those demands are never ignored.

There are those who say that a cell, when it is part of a
        body, is not an individual, it lacks the amoeba's freedom.
Those who say that do not know that they, and the amoeba,
        are already inextricably part of a larger organism, called
        Life; or perhaps they do not know that they are individuals.
That organism, that creature, of which we are each a part,
        is the biosphere, the living surface, of this planet Earth.
That stirring we all feel, that move toward group-consciousness,
        is the biosphere of Earth becoming aware of its existence.
It is being born.
We are waking up.

For what it's worth, the millenium is upon us.

Our responsibility, as individual cells of a living organism,
is to perform our individual functions as well as possible.
Our orders come from within; they are not imposed from without.
We are free to be ourselves, as fully as we can; and the more
we are ourselves, the better we will be functioning, and the
more satisfaction we will feel.
Our lives will grow richer and richer as the health of the
total organism improves.
Our destiny is unimaginably high.

At the depths of despair, nothing matters, I can't do anything, got to get out of here, walls falling in, throw me a rope, I can't move, can't stand it, nothing, throw me a rope. . .

And one day, like any other day, finally tired of waiting for help that never comes, make a rope, tie it to a rock throw it up pull yourself out and walk away. . .

And it took all that time
    just to find yourself.

And that's how long it had to take;
    and it was well worth every moment.

You hesitate, you think and struggle and finally you don't
even think about it any more, you just lie there in defeat,
you just lie there forever
          and then one day you get up and do what you have to
do, and go on along to the next thing.

The act of will is the creative act, the generative force,
things at a distance seem different than what's nearby so we
have the word God for the force that created life somewhere long ago,
distant, In the Beginning, and we get confused, perhaps
we also call it God that created man, that creature so inexplicably
different from other creatures, perhaps we even call it God or son
of God that walked on Earth and altered consciousness two thousand
years ago, always God is off in the distance, the creative force is
something in the past, we do not yet see the past as a time that once
was present, or the present as what will be visible as past, now, it's all
the same, our scientists looking into the microscope, the telescope,
looking into the very large, the very small, find things that only
numbers can describe, Quantum Theory, Planck's Constant, they can
find no words to describe light, words out of human language,
human experience, only equations to define relationships, working at
arm's length, the abstract, distance, why can't we bring it home,
things look different at a distance, the horizon, distant stars, the
curved universe, relativity, it doesn't make sense, Heisenberg,
uncertainty, the limits of observation, God is dead, meaning He
doesn't seem to exist in the present, here, the speed of light, a
number, light a particle, light a wave, energy, it's all energy, God is
love, what does that mean?, Newton's laws breaking down, ancestor
worship breaking down, free enterprise breaking down, it doesn't
work, God is dead, anarchy, Big Bang theory of the origin of the
universe, Steady State theory, where are all these subatomic
particles coming from, where am I, who am I, who is man, how does
he fit into all this, the universe is a creation of the mind, a function
of the perceptions, philosophers have proved it, science proved it, but
what is all this stuff man can't perceive, ultra-violet, infra-red, the
closer you look at it the further away it gets, all this effort to under-
stand the universe and what does it get us? the atom bomb, security

clearances, nobody believes any more, lost our faith, no faith in God the creator, no faith in Christ the saviour, no faith in the free market, no faith in the working class, no faith in science, no faith in technology, no faith in governments, no faith in money, do we dare to have faith in each other?

. . .Ah, wait a minute. Faith in each other. The act of will is the creative act, the generative force. How did life start on this planet? Answer: you can't stop life. Time is no object. Life just waited and waited and one day got up and did it and went on to the next thing. Ridiculous? Try an experiment. Try doing nothing. Do it as long as you can, do it until you *have to* do something, you can't stop it, you can't help it, it may take a long time, time is no object, I can wait forever, I've got time. Time is a concept. Life is real. It creates itself. Will. The generative force. God the Creator. Origin of life. What is life? Life is. Try and stop it. Try an experiment. Set off the Bomb. Uncertainty. Difficult experiment to observe. Nevertheless, outcome certain. You can't stop life. Cut off an arm. A leg. Blow it up. Wait. It grows back. Damnedest stuff. How does it work? Let's figure it out. Here we go again. . . What is God? You are God. I am God. What am I? I am Life. I am the voice of Life. *I* am the voice of life. Me too. Life has many voices. Life has only one voice. Listen to me. This is God speaking. Here and now, boys. Right here in this room. Right here on this planet. No distance. *NO DISTANCE???* No microscopes, telescopes, television cameras, priests, no protective glass, no underarm deodorant, no code of ethics, no standards of behavior, no laws, no society, no axioms? No Distance??? Get back, it's not safe, this thing could blow at any minute, who cares, I don't give a fuck, let's enjoy it while it lasts. While we last. Here and now.

God is what is there when you take away the distance.

All human consciousness is moving towards this awareness.
No field of human endeavor will fail to be revolutionized
    by it.
We're all going to meet in the present.

You can't stop life.
The Law of Conservation of Energy.

Memo to the human race:
if you can't lick 'em, join 'em.

Those who think man unimportant because of the vastness of space fail to realize that man is as much bigger than the smallest stuff he can perceive as he is smaller than the biggest stuff he can perceive.

Those who think man important because he is so neatly in the middle of things fail to realize that *every*thing is right smack dab in the middle of its own range of perception.

If you could look infinitely far forward in time, if you could look infinitely far out into space, there is no question what you would see:

You would see the back of your head.

Everybody wants to know,
    What can I do? We all want to save the planet,
pick up the garbage, free our brothers and sisters,
stop war and bring the millenium
      but what can I do, seriously?

Okay, seriously:
    get to reality,
      get to your own reality,
        become yourself,
become incredibly high and real and influence
everyone around you with your vibrations,
    no matter how difficult it is,
      drop everything else and
      start doing the most fantastic, real things you
               can think of—
become yourself
get to your own reality.

Have faith in *your* ability to be
        don't try to be someone else, that isn't being
your mere existence will change the world
        don't hang around trying to figure it out,
be bold and direct and honest and energetic,
            you know what to do,
if you don't think you know, do absolutely nothing
until you do, this method never fails, pure
receptive leads to pure creative
imagine what you could be and
        don't hesitate for a moment

take everything that is strong in you
and put it to work
set it free
never mind what anyone thinks
take all your muscles
and stretch them to their limits
you'll amaze yourself, how good you'll feel
and how much good you'll do
just by radiating pure energy outward
—contact high the ultimate form of communication—
you are beautiful

be
be
be   !

become

commit yourself to a life in which
you constantly consume your own security
—forcing yourself to seek a higher
security, which you attain and then destroy
        in order to go higher still—
it sounds unbearably painful
but it's just growing pains
didn't you say you wanted freedom?
freedom is not a tv set and bank account
convenience, security, won't get you high
        won't even keep you safe
they'll consume *you*
        and you know it

security is quicksand

can it really be *any* one's ambition in life
to become one-half the couple in the life insurance ads?

security. life insurance.
how much are you worth dead?

more than you're worth alive?
hurry up and die, then

hurry up and be born again

open yourself to absolutely anything that
        gets thrown at you
            —including death, and life—

open all the way

don't worry about picking out the important stuff
just let it all get thrown at you
        and the important stuff
        will be what hits you

all you have to do is not shut anything out

security is a glass wall
full security is a glass case that keeps
out all happiness, pain, awareness, change,
love, danger, truth
                and air
tear down the walls
        before you suffocate

tear down the walls
we should be together
it isn't safe
it might be fun

let go of everything you're holding onto

now let go of everything else

we can learn to stop struggling
by realizing we're naturally bouyant
if we relax (and persevere) we cannot
drown

abandon all security
you have nothing to lose but your chains

stop clinging

set yourself free

This is the truth.
It's all true.
Every word that anyone ever tells you is true.
If you could just open far enough,
make the effort to understand.
It is time to destroy the myth of the artist.
We are all artists.
We need to become better art *appreciators*.
There's plenty of great creation.
We need great listeners, great readers, great perceivers.
Great receptors.
It's all true; what's hard is not *saying* truth but
accepting truth.
Embracing truth.
That is greatness.
Open up.

Don't seek beauty.
Find beauty.

All life, day to day and century to century, is a succession of pride and humility, humility leading to greater awareness, greater awareness leading to greater achievement, great achievement leading to pride, pride breeding blindness, lack of awareness, imbalance, downfall and a slow return of humility. . .

Maybe now that we're aware of this cycle
  we can transcend it. . .
Is it possible to be high all the time and not get
cocky about that accomplishment?
It is if you really stay high. . .

Remember, but for the grace of God,
we would not be God.
It's something to think about.

The end of the world (heat-death of the universe)
and the moment of creation (in the beginning)
are illusions caused by looking into the distance,
like parallel lines that seem to meet (and stop,
or start) at the horizon.

Creation (birth, death) is a continual process
that happens in the present; the ability to come
into being is an inherent quality of life, it
is not caused by any outside agent.

Preventing conception/birth is not so easy as
arrogant man may think. (Whether it should or
shouldn't be prevented is a meaningless question;
at each moment you know what you have to do; wrong-
or-right has ceased to exist in our conceptual
universe.)

Life goes on.

Make things happen.
Let things happen.

If someone wants to love you and you
won't let them, what does that mean?

thought: I can't.
awareness: I can do anything I want.

thought: I don't want to.
thought: Why not?

awareness: I am afraid.
　　　　I am afraid of the commitment, getting involved.

thought: But I am not always afraid. Or I am, but I love
　　　　anyway. Because I want the person bad enough to
　　　　overcome my fear or hesitation. I care enough to
　　　　try. Or I am possessed; the spirit moves me to love
　　　　and I do not stop to reason. Those times are easiest
　　　　—and most exciting.

awareness: You get what you need.

thought: I am limited by my fears.

awareness: I cannot eliminate all my fears at once,
but I can push them back, I can be braver,
I can expand my universe.

thought: I want to love more, be loved more.

awareness: I must open myself, must be willing to
take on greater commitment. The more involved
I dare get, the more love I'll be able to
share. I must work on my self-confidence. It
is the self that loves, not the body, not the
mind.

We must open our selves.

We must free ourselves from the patterns that constrain us.
There are two ways of doing this: fasting, and feasting.
Stop watching television, or watch it day and night until
your mind snaps completely.
Stop listening to records, or listen to records to the
exclusion of all else until it drives you mad.
If your fast isn't getting you high, isn't changing your life
and thought-patterns, expand it, limit yourself further, take
on greater challenges of deprivation until you're desperate
enough to see the light.
If your feast isn't getting you high, speed it up, overload
more and more, strain your senses to the limits and beyond the
limits, build on the tower till it topples, take in more and
more stimuli till you crack under the strain and break through.
The goal is renewed awareness, freedom; we can make it if
we try.

Repetition deadens awareness.
Repetition deadens awareness.
Break the glass.
Break the glass.
Don't think twice, it's all right.

Technology is a riddle that has us all puzzled.
The more you examine modern technology the more you find
damage to the Earth's living environment behind its
every extension.
And since we need to go on living more than we need the
technology, that seems to argue that the technology should
be eradicated.
A short-sighted viewpoint.
What is actually necessary is that we make a technological
advance.
This is not a trivial matter of correction, of course; we
are not talking about installing air pollution control devices;
we are not talking about reform; we are talking about revolution.
Bringing our technology up-to-date with our awareness will
require drastic conceptual changes in almost all complex
equipment now in use.
(An ax is a simple tool; coupled with awareness, it is not
destructive of the environment.
A chainsaw is a complex tool; it's too easy; it tends to weaken
the awareness of its user; in addition, it requires fossil fuels, which
are destructive to earth and water when obtained, and harmful to
air and life when burned.
It may further be noted that our supply of fossil fuels and
many metals is almost exhausted, etc. etc.
Similar comparisons can be made between such simple and complex
tools as bicycles and automobiles, abaci and computers, etc.)
Bringing our technology up to the level of our awareness
is the absolute, unavoidable complement of bringing our awareness
up to the level of our technology, which is where we've been
focusing our energy.
Awareness and technology meet in the life-style of the
individual; that is the arena of conflict and change.

All complex technology must be reworked so that no machine operates outside of the flow of life on earth.
Preserving the health of that total organism—*not of the individual* —must be the first goal of all our endeavors.
When all tools are designed and used with that in mind, man's technology will have advanced satisfactorily into the present. Until then, it is criminally inadequate, and must be destroyed in order to hasten its rebirth. That is the creative process.

Let's get to work.

Man's present technology is not a mistake—it is not possible to make a mistake—rather it is an extremely primitive precursor of the incredible organic technology that it is man's destiny to construct/create in this universe.

We must not let our primitive playthings restrict our creative genius!

We must not cling to the past when there is so much to do in the present.

If you would set to work creating the new technology, abandon all complex tools. They are misconceptions. All the brilliant discoveries and inventions of our times will be made with our minds and hands and senses, aided by simple tools and concepts.

This is true now as it has been true throughout history.

Many of the greatest discoveries of our times will be made
by those who, in addition to listening to their hearts and
to each other, listen to the rest of the kingdom of life:
to the trees, birds, insects, fishes, worms, algae; to the
oceans and forests and mountains and deserts and skies; to
all consciousness that dwells on this planet; to all of
life, not man's fragmentary awareness alone.

Get to know the beautiful, if you would
become acquainted with truth.

Get to know the truthful, if you would become acquainted with beauty.

The kingdom of heaven is within us.
All we have to do is find our selves, express our selves,
manifest our selves, and we'll find it all around us.
Why wait any longer. . .?

Refuse to have *anything* to do with *any* thing (like a nation or person or corporation) that seeks to grow wealthier rather than healthier, larger rather than truer. Do nothing to contribute to that cancerous growth. Isolate it. Let it die.

Energy is what fills the universe
Energy is what comes and goes
Consciousness is what defines the energy
Under that consciousness we're each in touch with all of it.

Under means within.

Truth is found within.

And bringing it to consciousness
is the act of creation.

Love is the affirmation of energy
that keeps it flowing through us.

Life is the self-creating energy creature we call God.

Self is self and all and alone and
responsible.

God help us all.

BOOKS BY PAUL WILLIAMS:

Practical philosophy:

Das Energi
Remember Your Essence
Fear of Truth (*Energi
    Inscriptions*)
Waking Up Together
The Book of Houses (with
    astrologer Robert Cole)
Coming
Nation of Lawyers
Common Sense
*How to Become Fabulously
    Wealthy at Home
    in 30 Minutes*

Hippie memoirs:

Time Between
*Apple Bay or Life on the Planet
Heart of Gold*

Collections:

Pushing Upward
*Right to Pass and Other
    True Stories*

Music:

*Performing Artist, The Music of
    Bob Dylan*, Volumes I & II
*Brian Wilson & the Beach Boys
    —How Deep Is the Ocean?*
Neil Young—Love to Burn
*Rock and Roll: The 100 Best
    Singles*
*Watching the River Flow:
    Observations on Bob Dylan's
    Art-in-Progress 1966-1995*
*The Map—Rediscovering Rock
    and Roll*
Outlaw Blues
Back to the Miracle Factory

Other arts:

*The 20th Century's Greatest
    Hits*
*Only Apparently Real: The
    World of Philip K. Dick*

Edited by Paul Williams:

*The International Bill of Human
    Rights*
*The Complete Stories of
    Theodore Sturgeon*
(magazines: *Crawdaddy!
The PKD Society Newsletter*)

ALL in print. For a catalog or ordering information, contact:
Entwhistle Books, Box 232517 Encinitas CA 92023 USA
www.cdaddy.com (look for **Entwhistle Books** button)
phone or fax: 760-753-1815   email: EB@cdaddy.com